Little Red Hen

Story written by Karra McFarlane
Illustrated by Tim Archbold

Speed Sounds

Consonants

Ask your child to say the sounds (not the letter names) clearly and quickly, in and out of order. Make sure he or she does not add 'uh' to the end of the sounds, e.g. 'f' not 'fuh'.

Each box contains one sound. Focus sounds for this story are circled.

f	l	m	n	r	s	v	z	sh	th	ng
ff	ll	mm	nn	rr	ss	ve	zz			nk
ph	**le**	mb	kn	wr	se		se			
			gn		c		s			
					ce					

b	c	d	g	h	j	p	qu	t	w	x	y	ch
bb	k	dd	gg		g	pp		tt	wh			**tch**
	ck		gu		ge							
					dge							

Vowels *Ask your child to say the sounds in and out of order.*

a	e ea	i	o	u	ay	ee y	igh i	ow o
at	h**e**n	**i**n	**o**n	**u**p	d**ay**	s**ee**	h**igh**	bl**ow**

oo	oo	ar	or oor ore	air	ir	ou	oy oi
z**oo**	l**oo**k	c**ar**	f**or**	f**air**	wh**ir**l	sh**ou**t	b**oy**

Story Green Words

For each word ask your child to read the separate sounds, e.g. 'b-u-s', 'p-oo-l' and then blend sounds together to make the word, e.g. 'bus', 'pool'. Sometimes one sound is represented by more than one letter, e.g. 'th', 'oo'. These are underlined.

cart crops mill flour eat ground

Ask your child to say the syllables and then read the whole word.

farm|yard self|ish litt|le hea|vy

Ask your child to read the root first and then the whole word with the suffix.

seed → seeds greed → greedy ask → asked

harvest → harvested peck → pecking snooze → snoozing

bark → barked crush → crushed

Vocabulary Check

Tell your child the meaning of each word in the context of the story.

	definition:	sentence:
screeched	*cried in a loud, high voice*	*"Not I," screeched the selfish cat.*
tended	*looked after*	*Little Red Hen tended the crops day by day.*
crops	*plants that farmers grow as food*	*The crops got big and tall.*
harvest	*picking crops when they're grown*	*"Who will help me to harvest the crops?"*
mill	*the place where the crops are made into flour*	*"Who will help me to push the cart up the hill to the mill?"*
snoozing	*sleeping in the daytime*	*Then, Little Red Hen spotted Dog snoozing next to a tree.*
gobbling	*eating quickly*	*She spotted Duck in the pond, gobbling up all the weeds.*

Red Words

Red words don't sound like they look. Ask your child to read the words but if he or she gets stuck read the word to your child.

there	watch	tall	some
other	over	some	one
were	who	she	her
one	all	said	are
my	do	by	where

Little Red Hen

Do not read the story to your child first. Point to the words as your child reads.
If your child gets stuck on a word help him or her say the sounds and blend them together.
Re-read each sentence to your child to help him or her remember what he or she has read.
Discuss what is happening on each page.

Little Red Hen lived on a farm with a sleepy dog, a greedy duck and a selfish cat.

One day she was pecking in the farmyard when she spotted lots of seeds on the ground.

"Who will help me to plant the seeds on the farm?" Little Red Hen asked the other animals.

"Not I," barked the sleepy dog.

"Not I," quacked the greedy duck.

"Not I," screeched the selfish cat.

So Little Red Hen planted the seeds, all by herself.

Little Red Hen tended the crops day by day. The crops got big and tall.

"Who will help me to harvest the crops?" asked Little Red Hen.
"Not I," barked the sleepy dog.
"Not I," quacked the greedy duck.
"Not I," screeched the selfish cat.

So Little Red Hen harvested the crops until it was dark, all by herself.

Little Red Hen lifted all the crops she had harvested into a cart.

"Who will help me to push the cart up the hill to the mill?" asked Little Red Hen.

She looked all over the farmyard, but the sleepy dog, the greedy duck and the selfish cat were nowhere to be seen.

Then, Little Red Hen spotted Dog snoozing next to a tree. She spotted Duck in the pond, gobbling up all the weeds. She spotted Cat playing with a robin.

So Little Red Hen took the crops up the hill to the mill, all by herself.

At the mill, Little Red Hen crushed the crops into flour, all by herself. She took the heavy sack of flour back to the farm, all by herself.

In the kitchen, Little Red Hen mixed the flour and cooked the bread in a tin, all by herself.

Then Little Red Hen took the fresh, crusty bread into the farmyard…

"That looks good!" barked the sleepy dog.
"What a good cook you are!" quacked the greedy duck.
"You have a lot of bread there!" screeched the selfish cat.
"Yes, I do," said Little Red Hen. "Let's eat the bread, my little chicks," she clucked.

Dog, Duck and Cat watched as the chicks pecked at the bread.
"May we have some too?" they asked.

What do you think Little Red Hen said?

Now ask your child to re-read the story helping him or her think about the best way to read each sentence.

Questions to talk about

Read the questions aloud to your child and ask him or her to find the answers on the relevant pages. Do not ask your child to read the questions – the words are harder than he or she can read at the moment.

p.9 Who lives on the farm with Little Red Hen?

p.10 When little Red Hen asked the animals to help her, they said 'Not I'. Why didn't they help?

p.12 Little Red Hen needed help after harvesting. What help did she need?

p.13 Why does Little Red Hen take the crops to the mill herself?

p.14 Little Red Hen didn't ask for any help to bake the bread. Why?

p.15 What did the animals think when the chicks ate the bread?

p.15 The story doesn't tell us what Little Red Hen said at the end. What do you think she said?

Questions to read and answer

Ask your child to read the questions and find the correct answer in the story.

1. Dog, Duck and Cat said **"yes / maybe / not I"** when Little Red Hen asked them to help.

2. Dog was **selfish / sleepy / greedy**.

3. Cat was playing with **a robin / the crops / some seeds**.

4. Little Red Hen took the crops to the **farm / mill / barn**.

5. Little Red Hen let the **cat / dog / chicks** eat the fresh bread.

Speedy Green Words

Ask your child to read the words clearly and quickly – across the rows, down the columns, and in and out of order.

playing	fresh	may	bread
next	carry	dark	good
tree	greedy	farm	too
day	may	plant	next
cooked	seen	heavy	look

Read Write Inc. Phonics

BOOK BAG BOOKS

Little Red Hen

Set 6: Blue More Storybooks

1 Little Red Hen
2 The golden egg
3 Help from the air
4 A shirt for a party
5 Lost and found
6 A knockout show
7 Mercury and the woodman
8 The boy who cried wolf
9 The kite contest
10 Joe's nose

Use Set 6 Blue More Storybooks after reading Set 6 Blue Core Storybooks.

web www.oxfordprimary.com
email primary.enquiries@oup.com
tel +44 (0)1536 452610

www.oup.com

Read Write Inc. Phonics
Black and White Storybooks
Blue Set 6:
Mixed Pack of 10
ISBN 9781382048163
Mixed Pack of 100
ISBN 9781382048156

Read Write Inc. Phonics

A shirt for a party

Set 6 More Storybooks

Story 4

ir

Story by Karra McFarlane
Illustrated by Tim Archbold
Series developed by Ruth Miskin

OXFORD

Notes to Parents or Carers

Your child has been reading this book at school. Let your child show you how well he or she can read it.

If your child needs help, follow the advice in the small parent notes next to each activity.

Remember to praise your child's success!

OXFORD
UNIVERSITY PRESS

Great Clarendon Street, Oxford, OX2 6DP, United Kingdom

Oxford University Press is a department of the University of Oxford. It furthers the University's objective of excellence in research, scholarship, and education by publishing worldwide. Oxford is a registered trade mark of Oxford University Press in the UK and in certain other countries

Mixed Pack of 10
ISBN 978-1-38-204816-3
Mixed Pack of 100
ISBN 978-1-38-204815-6

10 9 8 7 6 5 4 3

Printed in China by Golden Cup

Every effort has been made to contact copyright holders of material reproduced in this book. Any omissions will be rectified in subsequent printings if notice is given to the publisher.

The manufacturer's authorised representative in the EU for product safety is Oxford University Press España S.A. of El Parque Empresarial San Fernando de Henares, Avenida de Castilla, 2 – 28830 Madrid (www.oup.es/en or product.safety@oup.com). OUP España S.A. also acts as importer into Spain of products made by the manufacturer.